Captive Beauty

Captive Beauty

Zoo Portraits by Frank Noelker

Foreword by Jane Goodall

Introduction by Nigel Rothfels

University of Illinois Press · Urbana and Chicago

Library of Congress Cataloging-in-Publication Data
Noelker, Frank.
Captive beauty : zoo portraits / by Frank Noelker ;
foreword by Jane Goodall ; introduction by Nigel Rothfels.
p.   cm.
Includes bibliographical references.
ISBN 0–252–02899–6 (cloth : alk. paper)
ISBN 0–252–07169–7 (pbk. : alk. paper)
1. Zoo animals—Pictorial works.
2. Captive wild animals—Pictorial works.
I. Title.
QL77.5.N624   2004
636.088'9'0222—dc21   2003012761

For Laurie

The most moving painting shown last night was, for my taste, Stubbs's "Zebra in an English Glade." The animal, brilliant in his black and white stripes, standing in beautiful profile, looked stiffly perplexed and lost among all the dappled greenery. A stranger in a strange land. At least he wasn't in a zoo.

    —Alec Guinness, *My Name Escapes Me*

Foreword

Jane Goodall

Frank Noelker's work makes a powerful statement. It is both beautiful and profoundly disturbing. He has captured, in this series of portraits, the very essence of the problem of zoos. For here we see "wild" animals who are no longer wild. In some instances the walls of their cages have been skillfully painted so that, at a quick glance, they appear to be large, spacious enclosures—in their natural habitat, almost. Yet the artwork, the painted trees and vines and flowers, serves only to render more heartbreaking their stark imprisonment.

This book is not intended as an indictment against all zoos but rather as a plea for greater understanding of the animal beings within them. And as field biologists provide zoo administrators and keepers with better knowledge about the needs of the various species in their collections, and as the public has become better informed, things are improving around the world. Enclosures are getting bigger, and more and more attention is paid to enriching the environment, providing stimulation. The better zoos in the developed world bear little comparison to the old-fashioned square prisons of the last century. In the Beijing zoo I saw giant pandas sunning themselves up quite tall trees, and an absolutely enormous aviary is being built—even bigger than the huge one in Tokyo. The old zoo in Entebbe, Uganda, has been changed beyond recognition—the animals lie out in the shade in large enclosures surrounded by trees and indigenous birds. There are still, however, far too many of the concrete and steel cages left, especially in Europe. And the inmates of many of the zoos in the developing world live in the most horrible conditions. If there is not enough money available to create the best possible conditions, then animals should not be kept. It is as simple as that.

To collect the images, Frank toured zoos in many parts of the world and spent days sitting, watching, and waiting for the shot that would convey the story of captive lives, the indomitable animal spirits that refuse to give up, clinging to the last vestiges of freedom within their hearts. Frank's heart was broken, again and again. And I understand, for I too have looked into the eyes of three-hundred-pound gorillas destined to spend the rest of their lives in small enclosures while human animals gather to stare and point. No fierce displays for them, no crashing through the lush undergrowth of their native African forests. And there are other eyes that haunt me: the eyes of elephants chained to the ground, of wolves, those wild, free spirits of the north, in small pens reeking of urine, and worst of all, the eyes of dolphins taken from the deeps of their ocean world to swim round and round and round and leap out of the water to catch plastic balls.

One of Frank's images especially haunts me. It is of the bear in his tiny concrete "pit," pacing to and fro between concrete walls, swaying his head. Alone. Boredom has given way to stereotypic behavior, and he sways his head from side to side. He has lost hope. Yet I saw bears rescued from a bleak prison such as this and was amazed at how quickly they adapted to their new large enclosure. I could sense their joy as they dug in the ground, searching for grubs and roots, and splashed about in their pond. But in the wild bears roam over huge territories. And they are free.

Of course, in so many parts of the world the wilderness has become a place of destruction and terror. Animals are hunted with guns, spears, wire snares, and steel leg-hold traps. Their habitats are destroyed around them. They are dying in their thousands, some to become extinct forever. In the better zoos, those animals in relatively normal groups in relatively large habitats are the lucky ones, for companionship does, at least, provide stimulation. But many are not so lucky. Frank's images convey the terrible crippling boredom of their captive lives and the utter absurdity of thinking that a few daubs of paint can make up for all that of which we have deprived them. I can never forget my first sight of Gregoire, a chimpanzee in the Brazzaville zoo. In 1944 he had been put, as an infant, in a bare, wooden-floored cage where the sun never shone. Alone. When I saw him, he had been there for nearly fifty years. Through malnourishment he had lost almost all his hair, and his skin was stretched tightly over his skeleton. You could see almost every single bone. So starving, so alone—how had he survived? Now he has been rescued, for the zoo was destroyed during the civil war, and he has the company of other chimpanzees and an outdoor garden, with grass and a tree and a platform. He is a very special member of our JGI Tchimpounga Chimpanzee Sanctuary.

Mostly, we cannot put zoo animals back in the wild, although some captive breeding programs do just that. But most zoo inmates will live out their lives in captivity. It is up to us to provide them with the best possible habitats—appropriate social groups and an enriched environment. They must serve as ambassadors for their often beleaguered relatives in the wild so that we shall be moved to help the species and the forests, savannas, wetlands, and other habitats where they live.

Let us hope that the day will come when the steel-barred cage, the concrete island, and bare, sterile enclosures of all sorts will be no more. Frank's work, with its implicit plea for our sympathy and understanding, will play a part in making this happen.

Introduction:
Animals and Zoos and History

Nigel Rothfels

One of the very first exhibits built for the new Zoological Gardens of London that opened in 1828 was a bear pit. Essentially a deep hole with a large wooden vertical beam anchored into the center, the bear pit was one of the most popular exhibits at the zoo and remained a central feature of the place until the beginning of the twentieth century. Much of the joy of the pit for its human visitors involved feeding the bears. As the animals climbed the "tree" in the center of the exhibit, spectators would throw food and enjoy the animals' catches. Of course, not every bear would bother to climb the pole. But even the most indolent bear, sitting at the bottom of the pit, mouth agape, could be amusing; visitors would simply compete to throw food directly into the animal's mouth. Enthusiasm for the pits was not limited to London, however. In fact, by the end of the nineteenth century bear pits of one kind or another were in zoos all over Europe and America (and some of these exhibits—see, for example, Plate 28—are still being used). Although the appeal of the pits was particularly widespread in the nineteenth century, their history stretches back hundreds of years. Indeed, the bear pit can be seen as a kind of holdover from an earlier time.

It might seem strange to begin this introduction to a book of contemporary photographs of animals in zoos with a discussion of bears in the nineteenth century. Certainly, bears are not usually considered the most exciting animals at the zoo. Wouldn't it make more sense to begin with elephants, giraffes, zebras, rhinoceroses, gorillas, or lions and tigers but not bears? In contrast to these other animals, in fact, there is something decidedly unexotic about bears. For as long as anyone could remember in nine-teenth-century Europe, bears roamed both the woods and cities. Some cities had long traditions of keep-ing bears in pits, and in every city, now and then, trained bears, in the company of their human han-dlers, had walked the streets, dancing and performing other tricks. Indeed, by the time the great public zoological gardens began to be built in the nineteenth century, there was nothing new about bears.

But then we are stuck with a question. If bears and their pits were so familiar, why did they come to occupy a central place in the plans for the new zoological gardens—places that were supposed to show people something new and exciting? In fact, as the public zoos of the nineteenth century began to be constructed, it seems that almost no place wanted to be without an old-style bear pit. When Berlin opened its zoological garden in 1844, for example, most of the animals came from a private collection built up by King Friedrich Wilhelm IV. And when his bears were moved from the pit at his menagerie, they were moved to a new pit at the zoo.[1] The question about why bear pits, though, seems to be at the very heart of a larger question: Why zoos? At least a beginning of the answer to that question lies, I believe, in thinking critically about the history of this sometimes most perplexing institution.

Perhaps something in our nature makes us want to keep unusual, striking, comforting, or inspiring animals close by. Since ancient times, for example, people have kept small birds in cages. Indeed, the bell-shaped cages so familiar to us are millennia old and are similarly illustrated in ancient floor mosaics, medieval manuscripts, and today's pet supply catalogs. Why we want to have caged birds around us is a difficult question. But whether the desire stems from a vague atavistic longing for a life in nature and among animals, from a deeply rooted need both to dominate and receive unconditional love, or from some other cause, we've been catching and sometimes taming this or that animal for longer than history itself. Pick almost any historical time and place for which records of the lives of ordinary people survive, and you will likely find someone who kept a small collection of unusual animals. And when, because of increased wealth, power, or leisure, people have had an opportunity to expand those collections, they've quickly moved beyond local songbirds or small mammals. In ancient Mesopotamia, Egypt, Greece, Rome, India, Persia, and China there were large collections of animals containing the sorts of beasts we still hope to see in our zoos—things that were particularly large, dangerous, rare, or beautiful. Such collections are also evident in medieval Europe and in the Mayan, Incan, and Aztec cultures in the New World.[2] Not surprisingly, we have the most information about those collections assembled by important political figures. Indeed, the histories of early collections of exotic animals often read like a who's who of the powerful and are filled with names like Sennacherib, Ramses II, Wen Wang, Ptolemy II, Alexander the Great, Charlemagne, Henry I, Frederick II, Pope Leo X, Kublai Khan, Louis XIV, and Montezuma.

Beyond these great figures, though, are the thousands of small collectors or the impresarios of traveling menageries who managed to bring together groups of strange creatures, often at considerable expense. Of course, today it seems that almost anyone walking into one of the new super-sized pet stores can realize dreams of owning an extensive private animal collection. If buyers cannot find what they are looking for there, though, a visit to an exotic animal auction should fill any gap with appropriately spectacular hoof stock, carnivores, or birds. If a private citizen would like to add something more unusual to his or her basic collection of tropical or saltwater fish, llamas, emus, bison, boa constrictors, and macaws, the world of camels, cape buffalo, zebras, tigers, lions, and assorted primates stands ready at these auctions for often surprisingly little money. That the exotic pet industry has become so huge in the last century perhaps suggests just how much people have always wanted to see and keep unusual animals. In fact, the ability to buy and sell chimpanzees on the Internet seems to reflect both an ancient desire and a broadening demographic of potential owners.

Claiming that humans have apparently always wanted to capture and keep unusual animals is not the same, however, as arguing that the resulting collections have always had the same meaning. Indeed, from both a bear's perspective and a human perspective there are clear differences between a bear fighting for its life against a pack of dogs in an arena, a bear in a pit, a bear behind bars, and a bear in a naturalistic habitat. Those differences mark important changes in how we have thought about animals in captivity. The basic outline of these changes was developed more than a century ago by the first people interested in writing about the history of zoos. These writers, usually either directors of the zoos or members of the zoological societies associated with them, tended to adopt an optimistic and progressivist view of animal collections in which the history of zoos paralleled a more general history of human enlightenment.[3] Their goal, in short, was to trace the path that led from ancient collections to the modern (that is, nineteenth-century) zoo. And like the more general histories of Europe and the United States being written at the time, that path was seen as one along which the conditions of life, including those of animals, inexorably progressed and improved through time and through Europe.

The story usually begins with an account of the Roman Empire, where all manner of creature, from giraffes and elephants to tigers, lions, and humans, fought for their many lives against other animals and gladiators in public arenas. The history then continues and becomes a little less spectacular and gruesome, but no less romantic, during the thousand or so years between the end of the Roman era and the beginnings of the European Renaissance. During this time, beside large collections assembled by kings to reflect their splendor and mark their dominion over the world, one can find many smaller collections put together for less ostentatious reasons by monasteries, physicians, and a range of relatively affluent people.

After a thousand years of essentially stagnant development, though, the Renaissance, with its expanding nation states, increasingly powerful political figures, and renewed interest in natural history, saw a growing desire in Europe to keep exotic animals. By the seventeenth and eighteenth centuries these aspirations had led to the creation of, again, large royal collections of animals such as those of Rudolf II in Prague, Louis XIV at Versailles, and Maria Theresa and Franz I at Schönbrunn in Vienna, a zoo that celebrated its 250th anniversary in 2002.[4] Then, beginning at the end of the eighteenth century and through to today, the old, aristocratic collections were slowly replaced by what became known as public zoological gardens (although during the early years they continued to be called menageries). The key moments in this latest phase were the creation of a state collection at the Jardin des Plantes in Paris in 1793, consisting of animals confiscated from private entrepreneurs and aristocratic owners (including the few remnants of the royal collection at Versailles), and the opening of zoological gardens in London (1828), Amsterdam (1843), Berlin (1844), and New York's Central Park (1861).

The institutional watershed marked by the replacement of the old traveling and aristocratic menageries by public zoological gardens in the nineteenth century also marked an important change in how the animals were presented to viewers.[5] Typically, for example, in traveling menageries the impresario would show his animals to his audience one at a time. He would pull out a snake or point to a lion in a cage and regale the paying audience with the natural and legendary history of the creature. In many ways the typical aristocratic menagerie seems quite different. Usually constructed as part of the owner's formal gardens, menageries were laid out so viewers could enjoy the collection spread out before them like a fan. Royals at Versailles and Schönbrunn, for example, could look out over the animal collections, which were arranged as segments of a circle, from a central pavilion.[6]

Although there were often human guides for the many visitors who came to see these collections, the aristocratic menageries should not be seen as public spaces of education as much as private pleasures that could have political utility. In this way, they were similar to a personal library, greenhouse, or art collection. Although royal and traveling menageries may appear very different from each other, it is also true that the impresarios, kings, empresses, and others played quite similar roles. They all presented the animals to an audience in ways that would showcase their own remarkable knowledge, power, wealth, taste, or ingenuity. The menagerie, in whatever form, was intended to reflect and enhance the prestige of its owner.[7]

Much of the same could and should be said about the nineteenth-century zoo. It is true, of course, that typically the owners of these new zoological collections were neither aristocrats nor private entrepreneurs. The new gardens were usually built by a class—that increasingly educated, urban, ambitious, and commercial class we call the bourgeoisie—rather than by an individual. As such, the new gardens were not designed to reflect the power of a king or the talents of an impresario. Rather, they reflected such bourgeois values as science, progress, education, the extension of law and commerce (including colonialism), and the importance of public recreation.

Not surprisingly, therefore, the new zoological gardens were constructed in parklike environs where visitors could enjoy a respectable and entertaining outing. Visitors came to the zoo to see the animals, but they also came for conversation, an opportunity to listen to a concert, or to stroll down long promenades. In older zoos that have changed only slowly it is still possible to find the sort of long buildings, rows of cages on their outsides, typical of the period. Along these buildings the public could walk leisurely, pausing every now and then to look a bit more closely at this or that species and read the label, which gave all the information one really needed to know: popular name, scientific name, and country of origin.

A visit to a zoo in the nineteenth century was a visit to a park where not too strenuous outdoor activity, tea parties, and acceptable pleasure could be had against a backdrop of interesting animals. Much as we now seem to want to hide the presence of human invention in animal exhibits, the great zoos of the nineteenth century celebrated the presence of people and their creations at the zoo. Part of that was done in the very buildings themselves. In the exemplary Berlin zoo, for example, truly spectacular buildings were constructed for the animals and based on models from civilizations around the world. There was the huge Elephant Pagoda, built in supposed imitation of a Hindu temple and boasting yellow, brown, and blue domes with elaborate decorative tiling; the Ostrich House, designed to resemble an Egyptian temple, with paintings of "ancient" figures of men and birds covering both the interior and exterior walls; and the Moorish Antelope House, with graceful arches and minarets.[8] And at every zoo one could find small animals and birds housed in ornate, noisy, hot, humid, and often rank conservatories that had endlessly replenished stacks of cages. These were not the zoos we are used to today. Everything changed when a new kind of zoological garden opened in the spring of 1907 in Germany, and it is around the innovations of that zoo that the pictures in this book inevitably turn.

᠁ ᠁ ᠁

In the last decade of the nineteenth century, the exotic animal dealer Carl Hagenbeck of Hamburg, Germany, found himself needing more and more space for his stock of animals.[9] As the supplier of animals to zoos all over Europe and North America in addition to Africa, Japan, China, and South America, Hagenbeck wanted to create a new zoo or animal park that would be both a showroom for his wares and a new kind of destination for the public. After acquiring some agricultural land in 1902, he began construction on a zoo that would show animals in naturalistic landscapes instead of in elaborate buildings. On the one hand, Hagenbeck wanted to convince civic leaders all over the world that building a zoo did not necessarily require building elaborate heated buildings, and if places didn't spend money on buildings, they could spend it on animals. On the other hand, however, through decades of experimenting with different kinds of spectacles, including circuses and traveling shows of indigenous people, Hagenbeck had become convinced that the public would respond to exhibits that showed animals not from behind bars but in apparent freedom, separated from each other through carefully concealed moats.

More than creating a moated enclosure for this or that animal, though, Hagenbeck arranged his gardens so a succession of enclosures could be observed at once in a panoramic landscape. From a single viewing point, for example, one could look out across a small body of water to an apparent riverbank enjoyed by ducks, flamingos, and small deer. Beyond them, larger antelopes, ostriches, and zebras milled about, seemingly watched from still farther back by lions resting beside water holes or in the shade of "rock" grottos. Dominating the entire panorama, a rugged "cliff" provided habitat for wild goats and vultures. With his designs, he claimed, "Ibexes, chamois, and antelopes need not trust their lives in captivity to low cages, but rather could strive for the heights on a cliff-like ridge."[10]

Not surprisingly, ever since the opening of his animal park, historians of zoos have been in the habit of talking about the "Hagenbeck revolution." For a very long time, the bars on the cages had been a problem. As the poet Rainer Maria Rilke put it in "The Panther: Jardin des Plantes, Paris," written around 1902 or 1903:

> The bars which pass and strike across his gaze
> have stunned his sight: the eyes have lost their hold.
> To him it seems there are a thousand bars,
> a thousand bars and nothing else. No world.[11]

During the second half of the nineteenth century, more and more people were becoming concerned about the endless pacing of the large felines and bears, the depressed expressions of primates, and the intense smells inside the buildings. In contrast, Hagenbeck's park, with its open-air exhibits where animals seemed free to move about and mix with other animals, seemed a refreshing alternative. The public greeted the new park with overwhelming enthusiasm, and although administrators of the older gardens complained that Hagenbeck's exhibits were of little scientific value because it was so difficult to observe the individual animals, they grudgingly but quickly began to adopt their own forms of moated enclosures.

But the revolution of Hagenbeck was more than the moats and panoramas he created. The more important part of Hagenbeck's revolution was that he sought to convince the public that animals in his exhibits were happier than those in the older zoos, and he largely succeeded in doing so. Even though the animals in Hagenbeck-type moated landscapes were often given areas to roam that were no bigger than their old cages, and even though the animals were often shown in groups where individual ones might suffer increased psychological stress, the public looked out on the landscapes and saw Edenic tableaus. Those critics who saw zoos as little more than prisons were silenced. Before Hagenbeck, zoological gardens faced a more and more difficult struggle to convince the public that it wasn't so bad to be an animal in a zoo. Beginning with Hagenbeck, zoos began finally, and more or less successfully, to make the captive lives of animals seem less depressing.

At the same time that animals in zoos began to leave their cages and enter naturalistic landscapes, visitors slowly faded from public view. That is, although the public continued to be centrally important to zoos—the raison d'être of zoos remained serving the public good— designers increasingly sought to downplay large public areas and create settings where visitors might believe they had stepped into some wild place. Inexorably, picnic and restaurant areas began to move to the literal and conceptual peripheries of zoos. Whereas nineteenth-century photographs or paintings essentially always showed the public standing before or reaching out to feed animals, fewer and fewer people appeared in images of zoos during the twentieth century as photographers sought to make the animals in their pictures look as if they were not in a zoo. Even when an animal, in fact, was born at a zoo and spent its entire life in an old-style cage, official photographs carefully avoided showing the cage's bars and sought to catch the creature in that perfect, somehow believable, pose, standing before new, often fantastic, painted backgrounds.[12] In different ways, zoo designers, photographers, and visitors all participated in creating the visual fiction that zoo animals were somehow not wholly captive.

The reasons that bars and animal happiness became such issues for zoos near the end of the nineteenth century are many, and they stem from the same sort of thinking that brought a slow end to bear pits. One strong force was undoubtedly widely held, largely sentimental ideas about nature and animal life in the wild—the sort of ideas behind the rage at the time for stuffed toy animals and the stories of Ernest Thompson Seton. There were other pressures as well. It is clear, for example, that many who criticized cages had drawn their ideas from the humane movement, which had grown substantially during the nineteenth century. For many of these people, the issues of animals suffering in captivity—and the effect on the public of witnessing that suffering—would become the cornerstones of campaigns that continue to this day. At another end of the spectrum, however, were other critics, including a number of big-game hunters who felt that animals in cages gave the public an inauthentic experience. Zoo animals were somehow not "real" or were in some important way lesser than the animals they sought out in the wild.

Beyond these largely external forces that brought changes to zoos there were internal forces as well. First, it seems to have been in the very nature of the institution itself to change. As more was learned about animals and their needs, as the technology of displaying animals improved, and as the resources for redesigning became available through income from ticket sales, more and more ambitious plans for exhibits were developed. Those exhibits brought in more visitors and more benefactors, and more money became available for further innovative exhibits. Moreover, by the end of the nineteenth century, zoological gardens had become well practiced in demonstrating both their civic value and fundamental difference from the old, aristocratic menageries, which, they claimed, were little more than base manifestations a ruler's desire to show off his or her power.

The sense that zoos shared in a more general and progressive improvement of society is captured well, I think, in an enigmatic feature of the bear pit in London. The story goes that the top of the "tree" in the pit was encircled with an iron band, upon which was inscribed the word *Excelsior,* a word which, according to Latin grammar, means "higher" but was widely used at the time as "an expression of incessant aspiration after higher attainment."[13] The word was most likely intended to describe the climbing of the bears up the pole. It also seems to describe the desire of the founders and developers of the zoological gardens to work continuously toward improving the institution and its role in society. That internal optimism about the purpose of zoos has been a consistent force in pushing designers and directors to take their zoos "to the next level."

However important these discreet forces were in bringing the end of bars and the beginning of naturalistic settings for animals in zoos, the most important force for change has probably been whether zoo visitors "liked" or "disliked" a particular zoo or exhibit. The reasons for these likes and dislikes are largely ineffable—at a certain time, for example, a bear pit was no longer the most popular exhibit at a zoo and became, in effect, so disappointing that it had to be completely removed. People just didn't like that kind of exhibit anymore. It appears that ever since a broad population started visiting zoos more than a century ago there have been both passionate detractors and devoted advocates. Today, enthusiastic zoo-goers see a zoo as a place of innocent pleasure, of education, and of science and conservation; it is a sanctuary and respite from urban stress. For them, the zoo is a wholesome place for a family outing. It is a place where concern and compassion for animals is made evident every day and where a group of people, who have what is often described as the best job imaginable, dedicate their lives to taking care of precious animals, some of which might be among the very few remaining of their species. It is a place committed to furthering knowledge about animals, both among scientists and the broad public, a place where important and unmatchable lessons about conservation can be taught. When I take my three-year-old to the zoo, for example, when I see his surprise at the polar bear diving into the water and swimming up to the window literally inches from his face, when I can talk to him about the lives of the animals we watch, and when I see him try to get his mind around the idea of an elephant, I can be glad that zoos exist.

On the other side of the debate, however, are thoughtful people who see zoos as places of horrible duress and exploitation, as prisons for animals where psychologically damaged creatures lead pathetic lives, pacing back and forth but going nowhere. For these people, zoos are at best a necessary evil and at worst an appalling kind of entertainment in which rare animals are bred only to increase ticket sales and where terms like "conservation" or "education" are deployed only to mask the true natures of these obviously commercial enterprises. One scholar has even taken this issue a step further and argued that the best analogy for a zoo is not a prison but rather a strip club—a place where the objectifying gaze, in a coercive environment, is allowed to see what is normally hidden.[14]

Sanctuary or strip club—with such radically different opinions about zoos it is often difficult to imagine that people could be describing the same place. One way out of this conundrum, of course, is to conclude that they are not. For a long time, in fact, we have been comfortable with the expression *better zoos*. We say things like, "While it may be true that some animals don't have particularly enjoyable lives in some zoos, the 'better zoos' build exhibits with the animals' needs in mind." The expression *better zoos* has even been reified in the United States through accreditation by the American Zoo and Aquarium Association (AZA). Such accredited zoos (208 as of early 2003) have become carefully distinguished, even in animal rights literature, from the typically more low-brow and ethically more dubious, smaller, private, or "roadside" collections that are not officially recognized by the professional association.

Generally speaking, real and important differences exist between accredited zoos and most, although not all, other collections. Perhaps most important, the accreditation procedure is designed to assure a high level of professional conduct and commitment to a rigorous and thorough code of ethics for the benefit of animals. Accredited zoos also tend to have more programs for conservation, research, and education and deploy them more effectively. It is only fair, however, to point out that there are many smaller and other nonaccredited zoos that could argue that they, too, make real contributions to conservation, education, and science and that their own codes of ethics are at least the equal to that put forward by the AZA. The line dividing good zoos from bad is probably fuzzier than we think, and something still sticks to the idea that a zoo is a zoo is a zoo. Still, if only on a gut level, we somehow do sense a difference—don't we?

To understand the nature of that difference, we have to return to Hagenbeck's Animal Park. What Hagenbeck understood better than anyone of his time was that for a zoo to be successful with the public, for people to be convinced that what they beheld that day was truly something remarkable, memorable, or significant, it is less important *what* is shown than *how* it is seen. With the exception of fewer than a handful of species, what kind of creature is actually on exhibit (that is, *what* is being shown) has rarely been a reliable measure of its potential success with the public. On the contrary, the impression that people take away from an exhibit—whether the animal seems happy, interested, and not somehow captive (that is, *how* the animal is perceived)—has always been much more important. A polar bear in one zoo, playing in a giant, blue, and obsessively clear pool where people can watch it from both above and below the surface, can be *the* sensation, whereas people at another zoo might walk past another polar bear with either indifference or feelings of concern as they see it repeating neurotic movements in a fake-rock grotto behind an empty moat. Similarly, despite initial enthusiasm, people do not tend to spend a great deal of time in repeated visits to the zoo watching koalas sleep in fake trees stuffed with eucalyptus branches. Give them the chance to touch a suitably sedate koala, however, or the chance to have their picture taken with one, and they are likely to queue for an eternity. Even an elephant can become ordinary for an audience. But have an elephant keeper working with the animal, giving it a bath or going through a training exercise, and the meandering public suddenly stops and watches.

When people come home from a visit to the zoo, they are often asked, "What did you see?" In most cases the answer comes down to a handful of animals, and yet they had probably seen hundreds. So, what about that handful of animals? More than anything else, I believe that what distinguishes a good zoo from a bad one, a good visit from a bad one, a happy visitor from a guilty one, is what happens in that handful of encounters with specific animals and the exhibits in which they were seen. In the end, the most remarkably recreated tropical forests would be of virtually no interest to visitors without the believable habitation of large animals in the exhibits. People go to the zoo to see animals, but their experience of those animals is importantly structured by the exhibits in which the animals are shown. For example, when I was caught in the literal downpour of a rainstorm—complete with simulated thunder and lightning—in Schönbrunn Zoo's new Bornean Rainforest, and as I, like every other human there, sought refuge under a broad leaf or slight overhang of rock, I chuckled like someone might in the fun-house at an amusement park. When I looked up through the trees, however, and saw a type of cockatoo, hanging upside down from a branch thirty feet above me in the full rain and bathing its belly and the underside of its wings with completely apparent pleasure, I experienced what a zoo can really do when at its best.

The good/bad dichotomy, with its changing measures—bars versus enclosures, commercialism versus education, and exploitation versus conservation—may provide useful yardsticks, but it may not be the best or most complete way of talking or thinking about zoos. Perhaps we need to consider them in a more subtle way as ever-changing kinds of institutions in which the ideas and activities of visitors, caregivers, architects, and the animals themselves contribute to the evolution of the zoo's purpose and appearance. At first glance, it seems reasonable to conclude that the quality of an animal's life in a zoo may indeed have something to do with how "natural" its exhibit looks to the viewer, but it shouldn't be hard for any of us to imagine exhibits that might appear miserable to us but are satisfying for a particular animal. It shouldn't be hard for any of us to realize that what makes an animal's life in a zoo more or less tolerable has a great deal more to do with the relationship it has with its caregivers than whether it is surrounded with all kinds of synthetic trees and plants that make the exhibit seem like some kind of wild setting.

What must become more important, especially as we consider the future of zoos in our society, is that visitors take the time to see and reflect upon both the animal and the zoo. In that process, moreover, people must realize that a zoo is a great deal more than just a few "better" or "worse" exhibits. It is specific animals with unique histories and manners; it is the keepers, veterinarians, and curatorial staff; it is the long-range development plan; it is the interactions between the volunteers and the public; it is school groups out for an adventure; and it is the fact that a particular zoo may be the only home that most of the animals will ever know.

What makes Frank Noelker's photographs so important is that they highlight the human environments within which animals in zoos live. Ever since people started taking photographs of Hagenbeck's panoramas and more recent naturalistic exhibits, most have tried to hide the human context and make the animals look like they are living in the wild. One of the reasons Frank's pictures are so provocative, I believe, is that he doesn't hide the animal's actual life. That life is his focus. When we can see a keeper's rake or the straight lines on walls or in wires, he makes it possible for us to see the animal, the zoo, and history in a different way.

By showing us the animal *in* the zoo, by showing us its life, Frank points to a critical element in the history of zoos that people rarely ever think about—the place of the animals in making that history. One of the basic questions that historians of zoos have wanted to explore over the years is why zoos do not look the same today as they have in the past. Different arguments have been put forth. Authors have pointed to brilliant ideas by designers, pressure by animal rights groups, efforts to improve husbandry, the changing world and local politics and economies, desires to give animals a better existence, evolving ideas about animal psychology and captivity, and more. Frank's pictures point out that part of the answer, perhaps a very large part, is that the expressions of the animals themselves have pushed people into thinking about animal exhibits in different ways. Beyond their deep aesthetic power, what affects us in Frank's photographs is that the animals (and the artist) are answering questions we all have about animal life in zoos. The answers are not always what we want to hear.

Although likely about his deteriorating relationship with his mentor, Rodin, and not about animals, there is another poem by Rilke that seems to resonate with the mood in many of Frank's photographs. The poem, written around 1905, is entitled "The Captive" and reads in part:

> Imagine all around you, skies and wind
> transformed to stone, the whole world petrified,

the breath you breathe, the light within your eyes,
your own small world, your living heart, your hands,

the words that you possess: *this morning, later,*
further off, next year—suppose those words
were to grow painful, were to grow infected
and purulent and never ceased to fester . . .[15]

In the late afternoon of a winter day many years ago, I had the opportunity to sit with a group of students studying the history of zoos; our location was a decommissioned lion exhibit in a small East Coast zoo.[16] The exhibit would be familiar to most of us. The lions used to walk about on a flat outcropping of fake rock covered with hard soil and a few bushes and boulders. They would look up, across a gaping and barren moat spanning more than 180 degrees of a circle, at the torsos of people looking back down at them from over a waist-high concrete wall. The people looked down at the lions; the lions looked up at concrete and listened to what must have been the relentless and echoing cacophony of people saying, "Ooh, look at the lions."

That lion exhibit—the more naturalistic descendent of the earlier bear pits—is the world described in "The Captive." It is a world that can still be found in many of our zoos. As I've said, one shouldn't try to gauge the quality of an animal's life simply by how an exhibit might appear to *us* without an understanding of the many particular features of its life and companionship with other animals and its caregivers. Nevertheless, I believe the willingness to experience the sort of empathy sought in Rilke's poem is, in large measure, what truly distinguishes those zoos that consistently ask hard questions about their practices from the rest of the animal collections in our midst. These more self-critical zoos are the places that try to do more than just make an exhibit look good to the viewer; that are more concerned with what their exhibits and their animals communicate to the audience than whether they have prestige animals like giant pandas, large sharks, dolphins, or koalas in their collection; and that work hard to provide for the psychological needs of more than just a few key species. The animals in Frank Noelker's photographs ask us to see them in their lived environments. They challenge us to think about why we go to zoos and why we think such places should exist or not. The answers to those questions are individual and complex—but asking them is the most critical part of being the humans at the zoo.

Notes

I am pleased to thank Tracey Dolphin and Narisara Murray for their thoughtful comments on drafts of this introduction.

1. Because the ground at the new zoo was too wet to construct a traditional pit, Berlin built its pit from the ground up within a "bear castle" so people could stand at the top of the building and still look down into a pit. See the description in Heinz-Georg Klös and Ursula Klös, eds., *Der Berliner Zoo im Spiegel seiner Bauten, 1841–1989* (Berlin: Heenemann, 1990), 30.

2. For a solid account of early animal collections, see Vernon Kisling, Jr., ed., *Zoo and Aquarium History: Ancient Animal Collections to Zoological Gardens* (Boca Raton: CRC Press, 2001), especially 1–37.

3. See, especially, Friedrich Knauer, *Der Zoologische Garten: Entwicklungsgang, Anlage und Betrieb unserer Tiergärten* (Leipzig: Theod. Thomas Verlag, n.d. [ca. 1913]); Gustav Loisel, *Histoire des Menageries* (Paris: O. Doin et Fils, 1912); C. V. A. Peel, *The Zoological Gardens of Europe: Their History and Chief Features* (London: F. E. Robinson, 1903); and Ellen Velvin, *From Jungle to Zoo* (New York: Moffat, Yard, 1915).

4. On the menagerie at Versailles, see Louise E. Robbins, *Elephant Slaves and Pampered Parrots: Exotic Animals in Eighteenth-Century Paris* (Baltimore: Johns Hopkins University Press, 2002), especially 37–67; on the menagerie at Schönbrunn, see Mitchell G. Ash and Lothar Dittrich, eds., *Menagerie des Kaisers, Zoo der Wiener: 250 Jahre Tiergarten Schönbrunn* (Vienna: Pichler, 2002); on the later Jardin des Plantes, see Richard W. Burkhardt, Jr., "Constructing the Zoo: Science, Society, and Animal Nature at the Paris Menagerie, 1794–1838," in *Animals in Human Histories,* ed. Mary Henninger-Voss (Rochester: University of Rochester Press, 2002), 231–57.

5. The big division in the long-held history of zoological collections has always been between what we now usually call a "menagerie" and the more familiar "zoological garden." Of the two terms, the former is actually more expansive and used to describe all those collections of captive animals kept largely only for purposes of display or for the aggrandizement of the owner. Thus, eighth- or eighteenth-century royal collections and sixteenth- or twentieth-century traveling or fixed collections of caged animals shown for profit are usually called "menageries," although small collections today are more likely to be called "small zoos" or "animal sanctuaries" because of the negative connotation of the word *menagerie.* The term *zoological garden,* however, is more limited and used to describe only those places that have been generally founded by public organizations of some kind and exist primarily to advance science, promote public education and animal conservation, and provide vital recreation.

Most of the larger zoological gardens built all over the world in the nineteenth century by scientific societies, limited stock companies, colonial organizations, and municipalities, or as part of the public parks movement, still exist. To be sure, some have declined markedly over the last century and have lost the sheen they once had (including such places as the London Zoo and the Franklin Park Zoo in Boston). Yet others have managed to stay at the cutting edge of zoo design and continue to attract millions of eager visitors every year. The enthusiasm for building zoos, however, has never really ceased, and major zoos and now aquaria continue to be built all over the world. Today, though, it is just as likely that a zoo would be built by a for-profit corporation as by a municipality, but even these more commercial ventures continue to claim that their mission remains rooted around science, education, conservation, and recreation.

6. In addition to Robbins and Ash, see Nigel Rothfels, *Savages and Beasts: The Birth of the Modern Zoo* (Baltimore: Johns Hopkins University Press, 2002), especially 25–30 about the Belvedere menagerie of Prince Eugene of Savoy.

7. See, especially, Annelore Rieke-Müller and Lothar Dittrich, *Unterwegs mit wilden Tieren: Wandermenagerien zwischen Belehrung und Kommerz, 1750–1850* (Marburg/Lahn: Basilisken, 1999).

8. For photographs of the Berlin buildings, see *Der Berliner Zoo,* ed. Klös and Klös.

9. For full-length accounts of Hagenbeck and his enterprises, see Rothfels, *Savages and Beasts* and Lothar Dittrich and Annelore Rieke-Müller, *Carl Hagenbeck (1844–1913): Tierhandel und Schaustellungen im Deutschen Kaiserreich* (Frankfurt: Peter Lang, 1998).

10. Carl Hagenbeck, *Von Tieren und Menschen: Erlebnisse und Erfahrungen* (Leipzig: Paul List, 1908), 179.

11. Rainer Maria Rilke, "The Panther, Jardin des Plantes, Paris," in *Neue Gedichte,* trans. Stephen Cohn (Manchester: Carcanet, 1992), 60–61.

12. For a particularly strong discussion of the origins of naturalistic displays in zoos, see Elizabeth Hanson, *Animal Attractions: Nature on Display in American Zoos* (Princeton: Princeton University Press, 2002), especially 130–61. See also Jeffrey Hyson's exemplary discussion of immersion exhibits, "Jungles of Eden: The Design of American Zoos," in *Environmentalism in Landscape Architecture,* ed. Michel Conan (Washington, D.C.: Dumbarton Oaks, 2000), 23–44.

13. My thanks to John Edwards, author of *London Zoo from Old Photographs, 1852–1914* (London: John Edwards, 1996), for relating the story of the word *excelsior.* The definition provided here is from the *Oxford English Dictionary,* 2d ed. (1989).

14. Ralph Acampora, "Zoöpticon: The Pornography of Preservation." Paper delivered at the conference "Animal Arenas: Spaces, Performances, and Exhibitions," University College, London, Aug. 20, 2002.

15. Rilke, "The Captive," 58–59.

16. My thanks to Rory Browne for inviting me to join this adventure with his zoo history seminar.

Captive Beauty

1. Hippopotamus, Washington, D.C., 1997

2. Monkey, Germany, 2000

3. Giraffe, New York, 1997

4. Leopard, Tulsa, 2002

5. Tapir, Cleveland, 1997

6. Monkey, Erie, 1998

7. Gorilla, Erie, 2002

8. Lion, Germany, 2000

9. Kangaroo, Fresno, 1998

10. Polar Bear, Germany, 2000

11. Monkey, Germany, 2000

12. Elephant, Fresno, 1998

13. Duck, Brazil, 1999

14. Peccary, Brazil, 1999

15. Lion, Los Angeles, 1998

16. Rhinoceros, Philadelphia, 1997

17. Meerkat, England, 2000

18. Owl, Germany, 2000

19. Deer, New York, 1998

20. Mandrill, Lansing, 1997

21. Tortoise, Los Angeles, 2002

22. Gorilla, Toledo, 1998

23. Dolphin, Germany, 2000

24. Warthog, Germany, 2000

25. Seal, Germany, 2000

26. Sun Bear, Philadelphia, 1998

27. Monkey, Germany, 2000

28. Bear, Paris, 1998

29. Red Ibis, Texas, 1997

30. Babirusa, Tampa, 1998

31. Tiger, Baton Rouge, 1999

32. Baboons, Texas, 1997

33. Rhinoceros, Texas, 1998

34. Stilt, Texas, 1998

35. Ocelot, Brazil, 1999

36. Chimpanzee, Germany, 2000

37. Hornbill, Boston, 1997

38. Seal, San Francisco, 1998

39. Lion, Brazil, 1999

40. Gorilla, Texas, 1998

41.   Zebra, San Diego, 1998

42. Lion, the Netherlands, 2000

43. Chimpanzee, Wichita, 2002

44. Penguin, Indianapolis, 1998

45. Monkey, Louisville, 1998

46. Seal, Toledo, 2002

47. Hippopotamus, Paris, 1998

48. Antelope, St. Louis, 1998

49. Orangutan, Memphis, 1998

50. Giraffe, Washington, D.C., 1997

Frank Noelker is an associate professor of art at the University of Connecticut. His photographs of animals in zoos have been widely exhibited, both in solo and group exhibits, and are included in the permanent collections of a number of museums. He has published a limited edition portfolio, *Animals.*

Jane Goodall, a National Geographic Society Explorer-in-Residence and founder of the Jane Goodall Institute for Wildlife Research, Education, and Conservation, is the recipient of numerous honors and awards for her work on behalf of wild chimpanzees in particular and the natural world in general. In 2002 she was appointed U.N. Messenger of Peace.

Nigel Rothfels is a historian and author of *Savages and Beasts: The Birth of the Modern Zoo* and editor of *Representing Animals.*

The University of Illinois Press
is a founding member of the
Association of American University Presses.

_____

Composed in 9.6/16 ITC Stone Serif
with Frutiger display
by Jim Proefrock
at the University of Illinois Press
Designed by Dennis Roberts
Printed in China by Everbest Printing
through Four Colour Imports, Ltd.

University of Illinois Press
1325 South Oak Street
Champaign, IL 61820-6903
www.press.uillinois.edu